The Magic Fishing Pole

by
Phyllis Hobbs

AuthorHouse™
1663 Liberty Drive
Bloomington, IN 47403
www.authorhouse.com
Phone: 1-800-839-8640

First published by AuthorHouse 8/24/2009

ISBN: 978-1-4389-7485-9 (sc)

Printed in the United States of America
Bloomington, Indiana

This book is printed on acid-free paper.

authorHOUSE®

This book was written for Dillon and Terry and is to be enjoyed by anyone who loves to fish or knows someone who does. It is dedicated to the memory of Bill and Pat Hobbs.   Thank you to my Lord and Savior for His inspiration.

I always have fun when fishing I go
With my Dad and my hat and my magic fishing pole.
Sometimes we catch fish; sometimes we don't;
Sometimes we walk; sometimes we fish in a boat.
I always take my magic fishing pole
                        to make sure that I have fun.
I always take my hat to protect me from the sun.

We always go to our favorite place,
           a pond at Uncle Ike's farm.
It has many trees, a peaceful breeze and
           nature is free from harm.
And I always have fun when fishing I go
With my Dad and my hat and my magic fishing pole.

One day my Dad said, "The farm is too far away. So we are going to try a new place today."

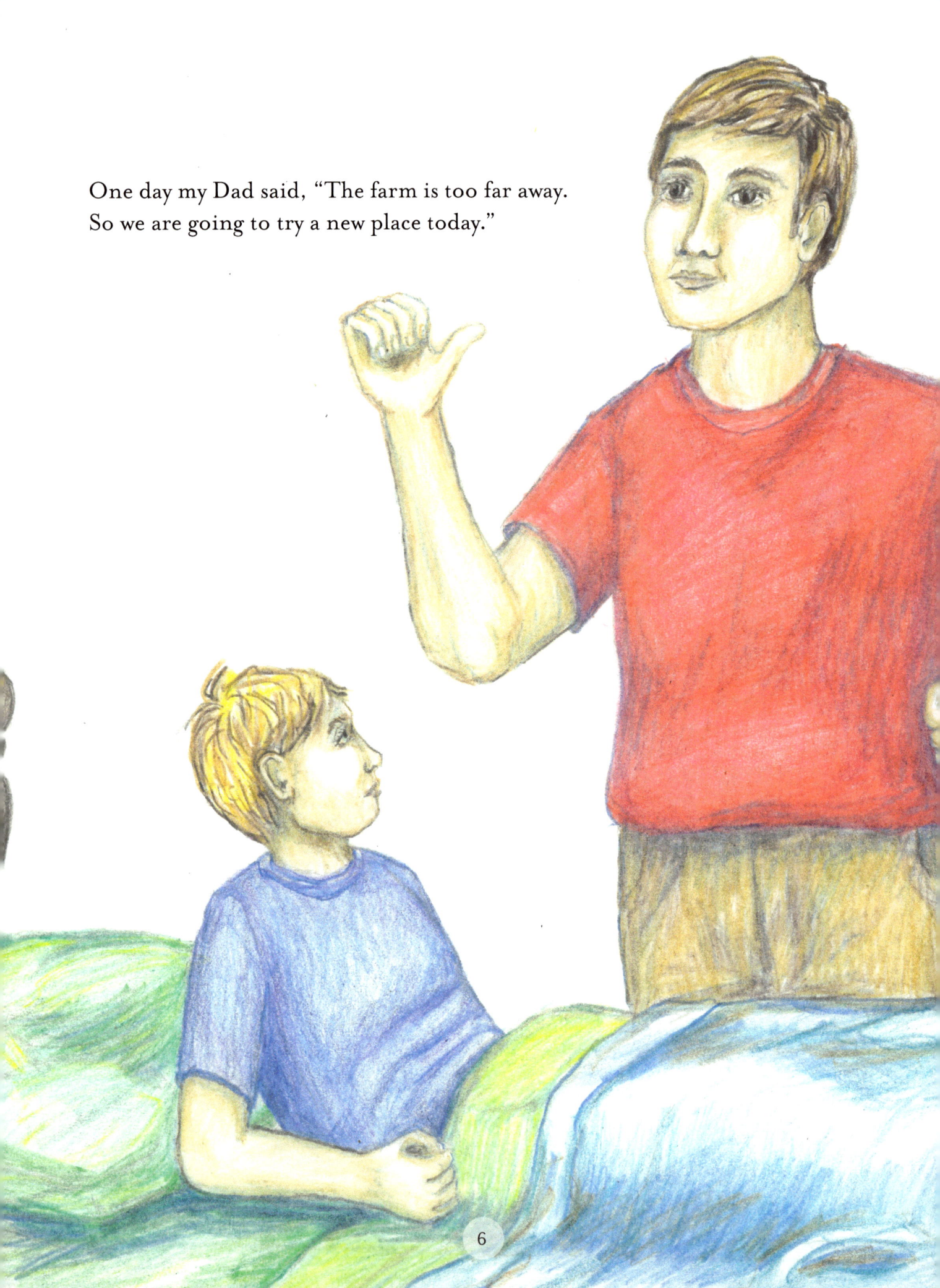

"But I don't want to go someplace else," I said.
"We've never been there; I'm going back to bed."
Dad just smiled.
        "You still have your magic pole.
It won't be the same,
                but you'll like the new fishing hole."

7

My Dad was right; we had so much fun.

And we caught fish until the
day was done.
And I still have fun when
fishing I go
With my Dad and my hat
and my magic fishing pole.

The day I lost my hat was a very sad day.
I sat in the house all day and refused to play.

Dad just smiled. "Remember your pole.
The day is quite sunny; we just have to go."

As we headed to our new fishing place,
My Dad was without a care.

But I was sure that without my hat,
The day would be too hot to bear.

I sat under a shade tree and
       refused to move away.
But when the fish started biting,
       I began to enjoy the day.

As I headed home that evening with fish upon my string.
I smiled up at my Dad and said, "Fishing is a wonderful thing.
And I still have fun when fishing I go
With you and my magic fishing pole."

One day I was practicing at an imaginary lake.
My lure caught in a tree and it caused my pole to break.
I thought my life was ruined and my fishing at an end.
My fun was over and my pole would never mend.

I used my Dad's old pole as we fished the next day.
The calm sunny weather lifted my spirits right away.
My hat and my pole were soon in the past
As I settled in the grass and made my first cast.

As the clouds started to drift,
　　　　my mind drifted too.
As the sun warmed my face,
　　　　visions began to shine through.
I remembered all the good times
　　　　when my Dad and I had fun.
I remembered all the good times
　　　　when we fished out in the sun.

19

All of a sudden my heart skipped a beat.
All of a sudden I jumped to my feet.
It's my Dad! It's my Dad! Now what about that!
It's not the place or my pole or even my hat.
Just my Dad and me wherever we go.
The good times just happen. Our love seems to grow.

When we returned home,
        more surprises were in store.
My pole and a brand new fishing hat
        were waiting by the door.

Grandpa repaired my pole.

Mom bought a new hat at the store.
And Dad said we could visit Uncle Ike's farm once more.

I'm going fishing once again with my hat and my magic pole.
I'm going fishing once again at my favorite fishing hole.
And though it doesn't matter where we go or what we take.
I am so excited; I don't think that I can wait.
Because I always have fun when fishing I go
With my Dad and my hat and my magic fishing pole.